Fitting In

Written by Ian Morrison

Japan

My name is Hoshiko. My family and I live in an apartment in Tokyo, Japan. At night we sleep on bedrolls that are stored in a cupboard during the day. Do you know why we do this?

Contents

Introducing Japan 4

Overcrowding 6

Privacy, Please! 8

Making Space 10

An Aging Population 12

Moving Around 14

Food for Thought 16

Japanese Technology 18

Energy and Pollution 20

Kids and Technology 22

Find Out More! 24

Index 24

Look for the **Activity Zone!**
When you see this picture, you will find an activity to try.

Introducing Japan

Japan is a busy, exciting island nation in the western Pacific. It is part of Asia, and most of the people who live there are Japanese. They have their own culture and language.

For many centuries, the Japanese people had little contact with other cultures. Other countries knew very little about Japan until the middle of the 19th century. Today, Japan combines the traditions of the past with the demands of the present. While many Japanese schoolchildren play baseball and computer games, they also eat traditional Japanese food and celebrate ancient festivals.

Japanese cities, such as Kyoto, are busy, colorful places.

Big, Busy Cities

Tokyo, Japan's capital city, has more people than any other city in the world. This chart shows the number of people in the entire built-up area of the world's five biggest cities.

Rank	City	Country	Approximate Population
1	Tokyo	Japan	28 million
2	Mexico City	Mexico	24 million
3	São Paulo	Brazil	22 million
4	Seoul	South Korea	19 million
5	New York City	U.S.A.	16 million

There are 125 million people living in Japan. The entire country is slightly smaller than the state of California, but it has more than four times as many people.

approximate   close to, but not exact

Overcrowding

Japan is a mountainous country, and most people live on the plains along the coast. As the population has grown, so has the need to find solutions to overcrowding. Japan has become a world leader in developing new technologies. In recent years, the Japanese people have used the advances in technology to come up with some very creative solutions to their problems. They have developed, and are continuing to develop, better housing and systems of transportation.

Tokyo has a large and efficient subway system, which is extremely crowded during the business rush hour.

efficient   run without wasting time, energy, or materials

Population Density

Although Japanese cities are very crowded, there is little crime. Japan has one of the lowest crime rates in the world.

The average number of people on each square mile of land is called the *population density*. The higher the density, the more crowded the place.

Place	Approximate Population	Approximate Area (Square Miles)	Density
The World	6,445,000,000	196,940,000	33
Japan	125,000,000	145,900	857
France	60,000,000	211,200	284
U.S.A.	295,000,000	3,718,700	79
Australia	20,000,000	2,967,900	8

There are still many places in Japan, such as this garden in Kyoto, where people can escape busy crowds.

Privacy, Please!

Traditional Japanese homes are well suited to a crowded country. They have many clever, space-saving ideas that also allow for personal privacy.

Many homes have special sliding doors with paper screens that light can travel through. These screens can be opened or shut to make bigger or smaller rooms. Tables are low, so people can kneel at them without the need for chairs. At night, some people sleep on bedrolls instead of beds. These bedrolls can be folded away during the day. In this way, the rooms and furniture can be moved around easily to create space or privacy whenever they are needed.

Many Japanese people want to keep their culture alive. Here a family is kneeling on the floor while they enjoy a traditional meal.

A City Apartment

A typical apartment in the city is quite small. This plan shows a home suitable for a couple with one child. The main bedroom is also used as the living room.

This space-saving hotel in Tokyo rents "rooms" to businesspeople visiting the city. Each guest has his or her own capsule with just enough room for a bed.

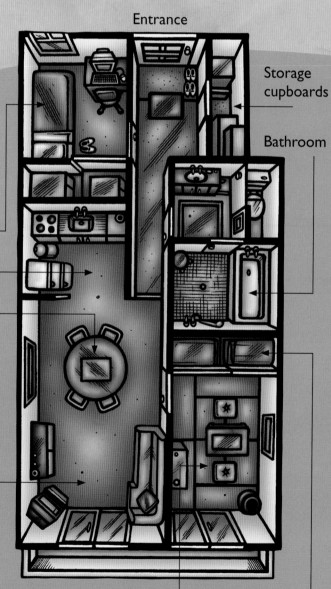

Entrance

Storage cupboards

Bathroom

Child's bedroom

Kitchen

Dining area

Entertainment area

Tokyo is one of the most expensive places in the world to buy land. Most families live in apartment buildings or very small houses.

Parents' bedroom at night; formal living room by day

Bedroll cupboard

Making Space

Around the world, high-rise buildings create extra space in crowded cities. Japan lies on a fault line, which means it experiences many earthquakes. Until recently, this meant that it was not safe to build skyscrapers in Japan. However, because of new building technologies and designs, stronger, higher buildings can now be constructed. Since 1980, all new buildings have had to meet strict earthquake-damage prevention regulations.

Some Japanese scientists think the answer to creating extra space lies in the opposite direction. They believe they can construct large, underground spaces that are connected by very fast subway trains. The surface above ground could then be turned into public parks.

No building can be completely earthquake-proof. Japanese schoolchildren practice sheltering under their desks so that they will know what to do if an earthquake strikes.

Activity Zone!

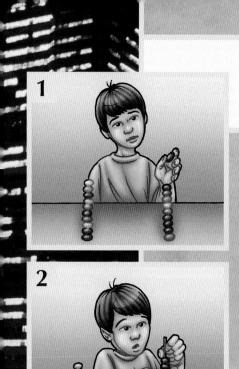

1

2

3

Skyscrapers are so tall that the walls at the bottom could not withstand the weight of the walls above, especially in an earthquake. Instead, many buildings have a strong steel frame, which functions like a skeleton, holding up the walls, floors, and ceilings. Try this experiment to see how a frame works.

1. Make two stacks of ten soft gummy candies. These are your buildings.

2. Give one building a frame by carefully poking a kebab stick through the center of each candy.

3. Hold a candy near the base of each building and gently simulate an earthquake by moving the buildings from side to side. What happens?

simulate   to model or imitate a real situation

Some seaside cities around the world have built up the ground under shallow water to create extra land. This is known as *reclaimed land*. It is usually very flat, so it makes good airport runways. Nagasaki airport, in southern Japan, is built on a reclaimed island.

An Aging Population

The average age of people in Japan is increasing.
Better nutrition and living conditions mean that many
Japanese people are living longer than they used to.
In fact, the life expectancy for Japanese women is
the highest in the world.

In the past, many Japanese families had a large number
of children. Traditionally, adult children took care of
their aging parents. Now most families have only one
or two children. Increasing numbers of old people have
no children whom they can live with, or they prefer to
have their own home. One of the new issues facing
Japan is finding accommodations for the increasing
number of old people.

life expectancy   the average number of years
people are expected to live

Population Pyramids

A population pyramid shows the spread of ages in a country's population. These pyramids compare the ages of people in Japan and Mexico. Look at their shapes. How are they different?

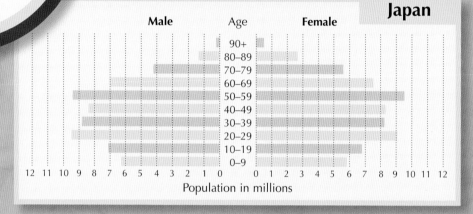

Japan

Male	Age	Female
	90+	
	80–89	
	70–79	
	60–69	
	50–59	
	40–49	
	30–39	
	20–29	
	10–19	
	0–9	

12 11 10 9 8 7 6 5 4 3 2 1 0   0 1 2 3 4 5 6 7 8 9 10 11 12
Population in millions

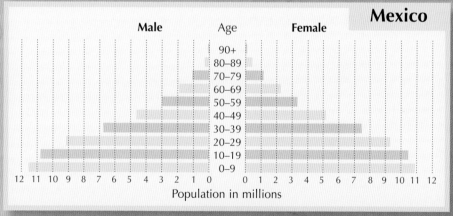

Mexico

Male	Age	Female
	90+	
	80–89	
	70–79	
	60–69	
	50–59	
	40–49	
	30–39	
	20–29	
	10–19	
	0–9	

12 11 10 9 8 7 6 5 4 3 2 1 0   0 1 2 3 4 5 6 7 8 9 10 11 12
Population in millions

Today, many elderly people are healthier and more active than they were in the past. These senior citizens in Japan are learning English so that they can travel to English-speaking countries.

13

Moving Around

Overcrowding creates problems for people wanting to move quickly from one place to another. Roads are often jammed with traffic, and many sidewalks are packed with pedestrians. In Japan, one solution to these problems was the creation of a modern, efficient transportation system.

The Japanese developed the world's first high-speed train system in 1964. The bullet train, or *shinkansen*, can travel at 186 miles per hour and has a good safety record. Japan also has the longest rail tunnel in the world. It stretches 34 miles and connects two islands.

Japan's bullet trains have electric motors in each of the cars. This gives the trains extra power and speed.

Modern highways and bridges connect Japanese cities, allowing workers to travel quickly from place to place.

Low-Technology Answers

With all of Japan's technological advances, the bicycle is still more popular than the car. For people in crowded cities, the advantages are obvious. The bicycle is—

- healthier for the rider and does not pollute the air.

- 50 times less expensive to maintain.

- often faster in rush-hour traffic.

- easier to park, taking up much less space.

- built using fewer resources than the car.

A bicycle parking rack in Tokyo

Food for Thought

Japanese farmers produce much of the food eaten in Japan. Traditionally, the Japanese diet is based on rice and seafood. As the population grows larger, these foods are still proving good choices. More rice can be grown in a given space than wheat or corn. Overfishing has meant that fewer fish are being caught in the ocean. So people have found ways to farm fish, shellfish, and edible seaweed in Japan's coastal waters. Japanese farmers are some of the wealthiest in the world. They make use of modern machinery, irrigation methods, and fertilizers in order to meet the growing demand for food.

Japanese farmers grow rice on terraced fields so that they can farm land that would otherwise be too steep.

Land for Farming

Only about 15 percent of the land in Japan is suitable for farming. The rest is either too mountainous or covered by towns and cities.

Japan cannot afford to grow crops that take up large amounts of land. This chart shows the amount of farmland available per person in some countries around the world.

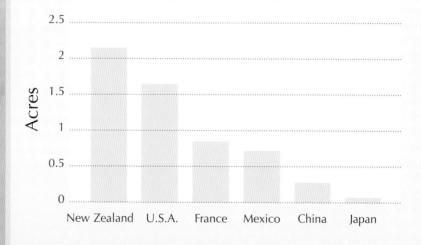

Available Farmland per Person

Acres

2.5

2

1.5

1

0.5

0

New Zealand | U.S.A. | France | Mexico | China | Japan

Families buy fresh fish from local fish markets and stores. Fast trains deliver different kinds of seafood throughout the country.

Japanese Technology

Many Japanese companies make money by exporting products around the world. In the recent past, Japan was most famous for producing iron and steel products, such as cars and ships. Now it is also a world leader in the production of high-tech electronic and computer products. Producing these items uses fewer materials and less energy than producing cars and ships, and they require less space to construct. Japanese industries often lead the world in inventing space-saving alternatives.

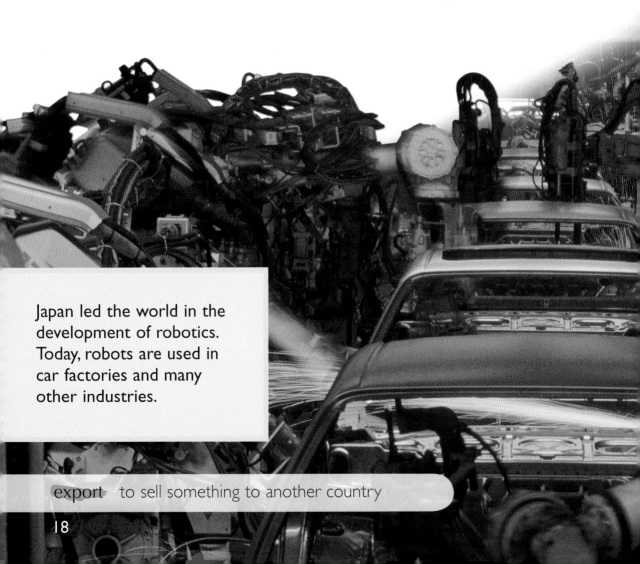

Japan led the world in the development of robotics. Today, robots are used in car factories and many other industries.

export   to sell something to another country

Made in Japan

Different electronic items are now being combined. For example, cell phones, electronic diaries, and digital cameras are often combined in one device.

Japan was one of the first countries in the world to produce mainly small-sized cars. Such cars take up less space than larger cars and use less fuel, making them ideal for Japanese conditions.

Japan also contributed to the development of transistor radios. These small, lightweight radios were first introduced to stores in the 1950s and were an immediate success. Before that, all radios were large and heavy. The transistor radio was one of the world's first small-sized electronic devices.

This cell phone can also be used to control a karaoke machine and song lists.

19

Energy and Pollution

Japan's advances in technology have come at a cost. The huge demand for energy has meant that 80 percent of the country's energy resources need to be imported. This is costly for the country. Also, like many other industrialized nations, Japan has a growing problem with pollution. Japan's main source of energy is oil, which pollutes the air when it is burned. The Japanese government is looking at ways of producing more of the country's energy from sources that create less pollution, such as geothermal energy—energy generated using heat from within the earth. These sources would not need to be imported.

Huge tankers bring oil to Japan's busy ports. Only the United States imports more oil than Japan.

import to buy something from another country

Alternative Sources of Energy

Wind is used to turn turbines, which produce electricity for homes and businesses.

Japan's National Institute for Resources and Environment investigates ways of meeting both the country's economic needs and its environmental needs. Some sources of energy that it is studying include—

- geothermal energy.
- wind energy.
- solar energy.
- gas from decaying wastes.
- artificial photosynthesis (creating electricity using plant chemicals).

Power station

Hot water in

Cool water out

In places where the hot, melted rock, or magma, inside the earth is closest to the surface, it often heats up underground water. This hot water or steam can be used to generate electricity. Geothermal power plants do not pollute the environment or use up nonrenewable resources.

environment the surroundings in which a person, plant, or animal lives

Kids and Technology

Education is highly valued in Japan. There is often a great deal of pressure on children to do well on school exams. Technology education starts at a young age. Most students have access to modern computers and are encouraged to take part in activities that use and develop technology.

Many Japanese children continue their learning in after-school or weekend clubs. These clubs involve children in anything from building their own robots to developing solutions to environmental problems.

These cub scouts are visiting Tokyo Electric Power Company. An engineer is showing them a machine part that reduces the amount of air pollution created by the power station.

Technology for Fun

Not all new technology involves sitting in front of a computer monitor. High-tech sports equipment and fun parks use technology to invent new ways to play. These children are playing in a "fog garden" in Kaga, Japan, where special machines produce a thick, swirling fog.

Find Out More!

To find out more about the ideas in *Fitting In*, visit **www.researchit.org** on the web.

1. Is overcrowding a problem in any cities in your country? What problems are caused by overcrowding? Can you think of any solutions to these problems?

2. What are the latest advances in technology that affect you? Find out what country these advances come from.

Index

buildings   8–11
education   22
energy   18–21
environment   21, 23
food   4, 8, 12, 16–17
housing   6, 8–9, 12
pollution   15, 20–21
population   5–7, 12–13
technology   6, 10, 18–20, 22–23
transportation   6, 14–15, 17, 19–20